SCIENCE FOR KIDS

39 Easy CHEMISTRY EXPERIMENTS

SCIENCE FOR KIDS
39 Easy
CHEMISTRY EXPERIMENTS

Robert W. Wood
Illustrated by Steve Hoeft

TAB Books
Division of McGraw-Hill

New York San Francisco Washington, D.C. Auckland Bogotá
Caracas Lisbon London Madrid Mexico City Milan
Montreal New Delhi San Juan Singapore
Sydney Tokyo Toronto

© 1991 by **TAB Books**.
TAB Books is a division of McGraw-Hill, Inc.

Printed in the United States of America. All rights reserved. The publisher takes no
responsibility for the use of any of the materials or methods described in this book,
nor for the products thereof.

pbk 5 6 7 8 9 10 11 12 13 14 FGR/FGR 9 9 8 7 6 5
hc   2 3 4 5 6 7 8 9 10 11 FGR/FGR 9 9 8 7 6 5 4 3

Library of Congress Cataloging-in-Publication Data

Wood, Robert W., 1933-
    Science for kids : 39 easy chemistry experiments / by Robert W.
Wood.
      p. cm.
    Includes index.
    Summary: A collection of thirty-nine simple chemistry experiments,
including "How to Remove Iodine from Water" and "Soap That Eats an
Egg."
    ISBN 0-8306-7596-5 (hard) ISBN 0-8306-3596-3 (paper)
    1. Chemistry—Experiments—Juvenile literature. [1. Chemistry—
Experiments. 2. Experiments.] I. Title.
QD38.W57 1990   90-49719
540'.78—dc20   CIP
                                            AC

Acquisitions Editor: Kimberly Tabor
Book Editor: Lori Flaherty   SFK
Director of Production: Katherine G. Brown   3596

Contents

Introduction   **vii**
How to Use This Book   **xi**

PART I   Experiments   1

1   *An Experiment in Volume*   **3**
2   *The Size of Water and Alcohol Molecules*   **6**
3   *Salt and the Melting Point of Ice*   **10**
4   *How to Remove Iodine from Water*   **13**
5   *How to Make a Salt*   **16**
6   *How Heat Makes Chemicals Change*   **18**
7   *Temperature's Effect on Solids and Gases*   **21**
8   *Expanding Gas*   **24**
9   *Testing for Starch*   **27**
10   *Testing for Starch in Toast*   **30**
11   *Testing Paper for Starch*   **33**
12   *Testing for Hard Water*   **35**
13   *How to Make Hard Water Soft*   **39**
14   *How Stalactites and Stalagmites Form*   **42**
15   *How to Make Bath Salts*   **45**
16   *How Soap Works*   **49**
17   *Soap that Eats an Egg*   **53**
18   *How to Make an Acid Indicator*   **56**
19   *How to Make Paper Indicators*   **60**
20   *How to Neutralize an Acid*   **62**
21   *How to Make Aluminum Shine*   **65**
22   *Making Copper Shine*   **67**
23   *Flexible Bones*   **69**
24   *How to Make Invisible Ink*   **71**
25   *How to Make Ink from Steel Wool*   **74**
26   *How to Grow Sugar Crystals*   **78**

27 *How to Grow a Crystal Garden*   **82**
28 *How to Make Carbon Dioxide*   **85**
29 *Carbon Dioxide and Fire*   **87**
30 *Testing for Carbon Dioxide*   **90**
31 *Testing Your Breath for Carbon Dioxide*   **95**
32 *Testing Unknown Ingredients*   **97**
33 *How to Separate Water*   **101**
34 *How to Make Oxygen*   **104**
35 *Rusting Iron and Oxygen*   **107**
36 *Quick Rust*   **110**
37 *Oxygen and Fire*   **113**
38 *Carbon in a Flame*   **115**
39 *Baking Soda Fire Extinguisher*   **118**

PART II Science Fairs   120

Glossary   129
Index   131

Introduction

The Science for Kids Series consists of eight books introducing astronomy, chemistry, meteorology, geology, engineering, plant biology, animal biology, and geography.

Science is a subject that becomes instantly exciting with even the simplest discoveries. On any day, and at any time, we can see these mysteries unfold around us.

The series was written to open the door, and to invite, the curious to enter—to explore, to think, and to wonder. To realize that anyone, absolutely anyone at all, can experiment and learn. To discover that the only thing you really need to study science is an inquiring mind. The rest of the material is all around you. It is there for anyone to see. You have only to look.

This book, *39 Easy Chemistry Experiments,* is the first in the Science for Kids Series, and explores one of the most exciting worlds of science—the field of chemistry. Chemistry is the science that deals with the composition, or makeup, of something and the reactions that produce changes in these materials. It is important to understand and control these changes so that new materials and new forms of energy can be produced.

Chemical change is all around us—iron rusts and coals burning in a furnace turn to ash, water vapor, and gases. Even the food we eat is chemically changed inside our bodies to give us energy and to make flesh and bone.

Our lives would be very different today without chemists and chemistry. Chemistry helps fight disease through the use of drugs and medicines. Our health has been improved through the discovery of vitamins and how our bodies use and store them. Many forms of fuels and types of energy would not be available without chemistry. Chemistry has helped to make it efficient to obtain metals from their ores. It developed new uses for iron and copper and brought about the discovery of magnesium, aluminum, and cadmium. Known metals have been made into important alloys with special uses. Ordinary salt has yielded sodium, chlorine, and other widely used compounds.

Everything in the Earth is either an element, a compound of elements, or a mixture of a variety of compounds and elements. A compound is made up of two or more elements. The same element will always be found in the same compound and at the same proportion. For example, pure water is always a compound made up of the gases oxygen and hydrogen. Oxygen will always make up 88.81 percent of the weight of pure water and the remaining 11.19 percent will always be made up of hydrogen. Table salt is a compound made up of the elements sodium and chlorine. Table sugar is a compound made up of the elements carbon, hydrogen, and oxygen. Baking soda is always made up of the elements sodium, hydrogen, carbon, and oxygen.

Compounds often have properties that are very different than the elements that make them up. Hydrogen is a very explosive gas when it is mixed with the oxygen in the air, and oxygen is a gas that is necessary for burning. Yet water, which is a compound that is made up from these two gases, doesn't burn and is used for putting out fires. Sugar tastes sweet, but it is made up of three elements that have no taste at all. A certain amount of salt is necessary for good health, but table salt is made up of two elements that are very poisonous.

The elements found in a compound are represented by their symbols. For example, the formula for salt is NaCl. The Na is the symbol for sodium, and Cl is the symbol for chlorine. Formulas might also be made up of symbols that have numbers. The formula for water, H_2O, means that water is a compound made up of two atoms of hydrogen and one atom of oxygen.

During the Middle Ages, chemistry was the tool of the alchemist, who was mainly concerned with turning base metals into gold. Today, it is in the hands of trained people conducting exciting research and making amazing discoveries. Experts are developing new alloys, plastics, and other materials for everyday use as well as new materials to be used in space. The field of medicine is also developing many cures for diseases through advances made in chemistry. The experiments in this book are an easy introduction into the fascinating world of chemistry.

Be sure to read the How to Use This Book section that follows before you being any experiments. It warns you of all the safety precautions you should consider before you begin a project and whether or not you should have a teacher, parent, or other adult help you.

Completely read through a project before you begin to be sure you understand the experiment and you have all of the materials you'll need. Each experiment has a materials list and easy, step-by-step instructions with illustrations to help you.

Although you will want to pick a project that interests you, you might want to do the experiments in order. It isn't necessary, but some of the principles you learn in the first few experiments will provide you with some basic understanding of chemistry and help you do later experiments.

Finally, keep safety in mind, and you are sure to have a rewarding first experience in the exciting world of chemistry.

How to Use This Book

Many of the experiments used in this book require the use of burning candles. It is recommended that a parent or teacher supervise young children and instruct them on the hazards of fire and how to extinguish flames safely. It is also recommended that children be advised of what to do in case of fire.

All of the experiments in this book can be done safely, but young children should be instructed to respect fire and the hazards associated with carelessness. The following symbols are used throughout the book for you to use as a guide to what children might be able to do independently and what they *should not do* without adult supervision. Keep in mind that some children might not be mature enough to do any of the experiments without adult help, and that these symbols should be used as a guide only and do not replace the good judgment of parents or teachers.

Materials or tools used in this experiment could be dangerous in young hands. Adult supervision is recommended. Children should be instructed on the care and handling of sharp tools or combustible or toxic materials and how to protect surfaces.

Protective gloves that are flame retardant and heat resistant should be worn. Handling hot objects and hot wax can burn hands. Protect surfaces beneath hot materials—do not set pots of boiling water or very hot objects directly on tabletops or counters. Use towels or heat pads.

Protective safety goggles should be worn during each experiment to protect against shattering glass or other hazards that could damage the eyes. Keep in mind that in chemical laboratories, for example, workers wear safety goggles at all times—regardless of the specific experiment.

 Flame or another heat source is used in this project and adult supervision is required. Do not wear loose clothing. Tie hair back. When handling candles, wear protective gloves—hot wax can burn. Never leave a flame or a source of heat unattended. Extinguish flame properly. Protect surfaces beneath burning candles.

 The use of the stove, boiling water, or other hot materials are used in this project and adult supervision is required. Keep other small children away from boiling water and burners.

 Electricity is used in this experiment. Young children should be supervised and older children cautioned about the hazards of electricity.

PART I

EXPERIMENTS

1

An Experiment in Volume

Materials

TABLE SALT
WATER
CLEAR DRINKING GLASS
TRANSPARENT TAPE
PENCIL
TABLESPOON

Place a small piece of tape on the side of the glass about half way up. Make a line on the tape for a reference mark (Fig. 1-1), then fill the glass with water up to the line. Try to be precise in your measurements. Next, add one heaping tablespoon of salt to the water (Fig. 1-2). The water level will rise about one-eighth of an inch (Fig. 1-3). Mark this level on the tape. Now stir the water and salt until the salt is dissolved (Fig. 1-4). This can take a few minutes. Let the water stand and notice the level. It will be back to very near the reference mark.

Salt is made up of tiny crystals. The molecules in these crystals merge with the molecules of water to form a salty solution without increasing the volume of water.

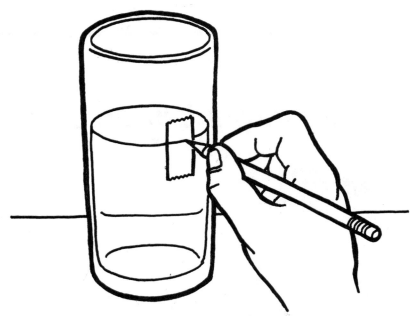

Fig. 1-1. Mark the level on the glass.

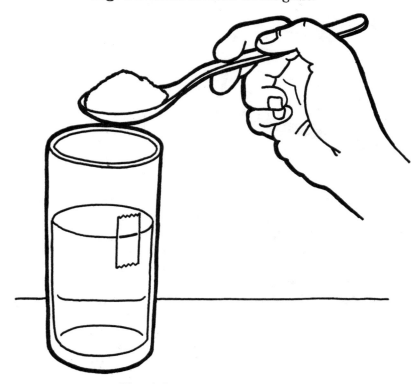

Fig. 1-2. Add salt to the water.

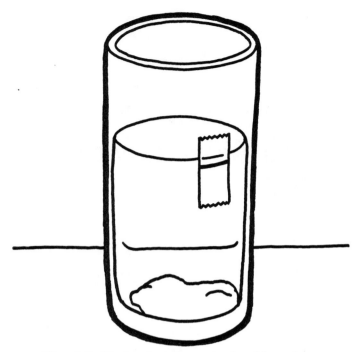

Fig. 1-3. Notice that the water level has risen.

Fig. 1-4. The water level lowers as the salt dissolves.

2
The Size of Water and Alcohol Molecules

Materials

2 JARS (ONE SMALL AND ONE TWICE AS LARGE)

TRANSPARENT TAPE

PENCIL

RUBBING ALCOHOL

WATER

Pour some water into the small jar and use the tape and pencil to mark the level of the water (Fig. 2-1). Pour this water into the larger jar (Fig. 2-2). Now fill the small jar to the same mark with water again and pour this in with the water into the larger jar. Mark the level in the larger jar (Fig. 2-3). Try to be accurate when you make the marks. Now, empty the large jar. Fill the small jar to the mark with rubbing alcohol and pour it into the large jar (Fig. 2-4). Then fill the small jar to the mark with water, and pour it in with the alcohol in the large jar (Fig. 2-5).

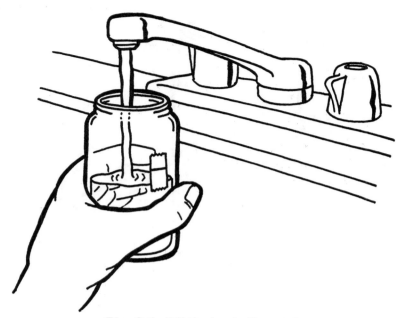

Fig. 2-1. *Fill the jar to the mark.*

Fig. 2-2. *Pour the measured amounts into the larger jar.*

Fig. 2-3. *Mark the level on the large jar.*

Fig. 2-4. *Substitute alcohol for one of the measurements.*

Fig. 2-5. *When water is mixed with alcohol, the level is lower.*

Notice that the level in the large jar is slightly below the mark. This shows that the water and alcohol takes up less space than water. The difference will not be much because of the small volumes used, but if one gallon of alcohol is mixed with one gallon of water, the result is about 3.5 percent less than two gallons.

This is because the molecules of alcohol fit into the spaces between molecules of water, much like pouring a volume of sand into an equal volume of gravel in a container. The sand fits into the spaces between the pieces of gravel.

3

Salt and the Melting Point of Ice

Materials

2 GLASSES
2 THERMOMETERS
SALT
ICE
WATER
TABLESPOON

Place a thermometer in each glass (Fig. 3-1) and fill both glasses with ice. Add a little water to each glass (Fig. 3-2). Watch the thermometers until both read 32 degrees. At this point, pour one tablespoon of salt into one of the glasses (Fig. 3-3) and notice the temperature of that thermometer. It should drop some.

As long as ice is melting in water, the temperature of the water will stay the same. But when salt is added, the freezing point of ice is lowered to below 32 degrees. This is how the ice in a home ice cream maker is brought to a low enough temperature to freeze the ice cream. Salt is added to the ice.

Fig. 3-1. Put a thermometer in each glass.

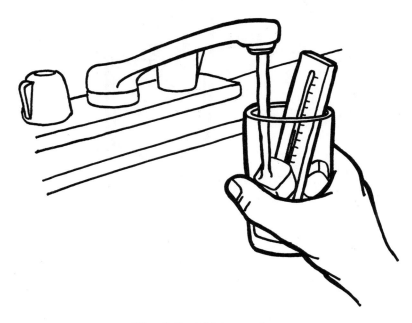

Fig. 3-2. Add ice and water.

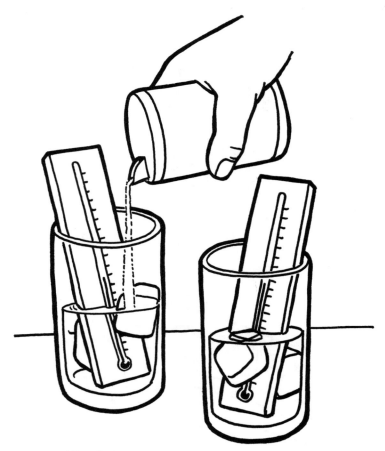

Fig. 3-3. *Salt lowers the freezing point of ice.*

4

How to Remove Iodine from Water

Materials

MINERAL OIL (NOT VEG-
ETABLE OIL) FROM A
GROCERY OR DRUGSTORE
IODINE
MEDICINE DROPPER
WATER
SMALL JAR WITH LID
TABLESPOON

Fill the jar about half full of water and add a few drops of iodine (Fig. 4-1). Replace the lid and shake the jar to mix the solution (Fig. 4-2). It should be light brown in color. Next, remove the lid and add a couple of tablespoons of mineral oil (Fig. 4-3). Replace the lid and shake the jar vigorously. Let the jar stand for a few minutes.

The solution will start to clear as the iodine separates from the water and is absorbed by the oil (Fig. 4-4). Most substances have a tendency to be more soluble, able to be dissolved, in some liquids more than in others. In this experiment, you found that iodine is more soluble in mineral oil than in water.

Fig. 4-1. *Add a few drops of iodine to the water.*

Fig. 4-2. *Shake the jar to mix the solution.*

Fig. 4-3. *Add a couple of tablespoons of mineral oil.*

Fig. 4-4. *The iodine is absorbed by the oil.*

5

How to Make a Salt

Materials

BAKING SODA

VINEGAR

TABLESPOON

SINK

Over the sink or over some paper towels, fill the tablespoon about half full of vinegar (Fig. 5-1). Now sprinkle the baking soda over the vinegar (Fig. 5-2). Add baking soda until the bubbling stops. The mixture has now become a salt.

The bubbles were formed by carbon dioxide gas. The vinegar was an acid and the soda was a base (a supporting ingredient). When you add a soluble base (able to be dissolved) to an acid you will get a salt.

Fig. 5-1. *Pour a little vinegar into a spoon.*

Fig. 5-2. *Add sprinkles of baking soda.*

6

How Heat Makes Chemicals Change

Materials

SUGAR
OLD TEASPOON
CANDLE AND MATCHES
TIN PIE PLATE
PROTECTIVE GLOVES OR
POT HOLDER

Put a small amount of sugar in the spoon. Spread it out with your finger so that it makes a thin layer (Fig. 6-1). This will cause the sugar to heat evenly and melt faster. Light the candle over the pie plate and hold it at an angle so that the hot wax drips into the pan. Wearing protective gloves or using a pot holder, hold the spoon over the candle and heat the sugar (Fig. 6-2). Soon, the sugar will start to turn into a clear liquid. Keep the spoon in the flame and the sugar will turn brown and begin to bubble. Puffs of smoke will bubble up and the liquid will turn black and char, or scorch (Fig. 6-3). Remove the spoon from the flame. Be sure to set the spoon on a surface that will not melt or scorch.

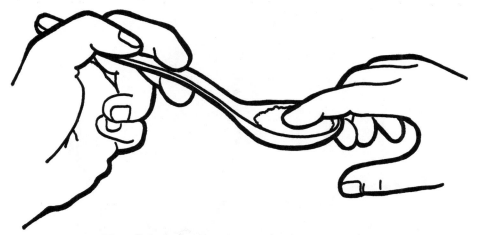

Fig. 6-1. *Put a thin layer of sugar into a spoon.*

Fig. 6-2. *Heat the sugar until it turns black.*

Fig. 6-3. *Heat changed the sugar into carbon.*

Sugar is made up of carbon, hydrogen, and oxygen. The heat from the flame changed the hydrogen and oxygen into a vapor that was bubbled away into the air. And the carbon remained in the spoon in the form of a charred, lumpy mass.

7

Temperature's Effect on Solids and Gases

Materials

GLASS
TABLESPOON
SUGAR OR SALT
COLD WATER
WARM WATER
COLD COLA
WARM COLA
KITCHEN CLOCK

Fill the glass about half full of cold water (Fig. 7-1). Add a tablespoon of sugar or salt, and stir the solution until the sugar or salt has dissolved. Notice how long it takes. Now, dump out the solution and rinse out the glass. Fill it about half full of warm water and stir in a tablespoon of sugar or salt (Fig. 7-2). Notice how long it takes for the sugar to dissolve this time. Dump the solution down the drain and rinse out the glass. Next, fill the glass about half full of cold cola (Fig. 7-3). Notice how it bubbles. Let the cola stand until it warms and becomes flat. Very few bubbles can be seen now.

The sugar dissolved much quicker in the warm water than the cold. Solutions made up of mostly water can hold more solids, such as sugar or salt, if the water is warm. If it were gases instead of

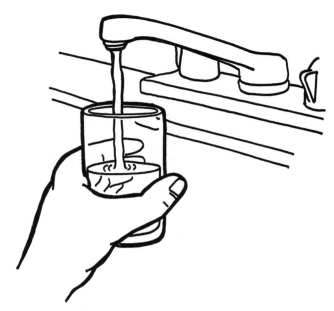

Fig. 7-1. Fill the glass with cold water.

Fig. 7-2. Sugar dissolves easier in warm water.

Fig. 7-3. *Bubbles of gas leave the cola as it warms.*

solids, however, the opposite would be true. The solution could hold more gases if it were cold.

When the sugar or salt, a solid, dissolved in the water, it became a liquid, absorbed heat, and lowered the temperature of the solution. So if the solution was heated, the solid would dissolve easier and faster. But the gas molecules in the cola solution began to move faster as the cola warmed and were forced to leave the solution. Heating a solid turns it into a liquid. Heating a liquid turns it into a gas.

8

Expanding Gas

Materials

EMPTY 2-LITER POP BOTTLE

COIN FOR BOTTLE OPENING (QUARTER)

CUP OF WATER

REFRIGERATOR

Put the bottle, without the lid, in the freezing compartment of the refrigerator for about 10 minutes (Fig. 8-1). After 10 minutes, wet the coin in the cup of water and remove the bottle from the freezer. Quickly place the wet coin over the mouth of the bottle (Fig. 8-2). The coin should be placed so that it forms a slight seal over the opening. In a few seconds, one edge of the coin will rise and fall (Fig. 8-3). This will continue until the air inside the bottle warms to the same temperature as the air in the room, or the coin moves out of position.

When the bottle was placed in the freezer, the air inside the bottle cooled. The air molecules contracted and took up less space. More cool air entered the bottle. When the bottle was placed in the

Fig. 8-1. *Place the bottle in the refrigerator.*

Fig. 8-2. *Place the wet coin over the opening.*

Fig. 8-3. *Expanding air causes the coin to lift.*

warmer air of the room, the cold air in the bottle began to warm and expand, taking up more space. As this air escaped from the bottle, it had enough pressure to lift the coin. When the pressure was released, the coin fell back down until the pressure inside built back up again. Cooling causes most things to contract. Heating causes expansion.

9

Testing For Starch

Place the paper towel or newspaper on a table or counter and put small amounts of each type of food on the paper (Fig. 9-1). Use the knife to cut slices from the potato and apple. Be very careful, and always hold the knife away from yourself. Never cut against your body. Pour a little water in the jar and add an equal amount of iodine (Figs. 9-2 and 9-3). Stir the solution. Now, using the medicine dropper, put a drop of the iodine solution on each food sample (Fig. 9-4). Drop the iodine on the cut part of the potato and apple.

Fig. 9-1. *Gather foods to test.*

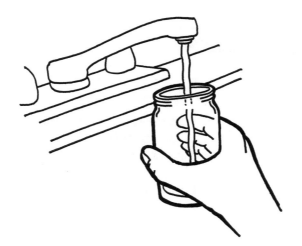

Fig. 9-2. *Pour water into the jar.*

Fig. 9-3. *Add an equal amount of iodine.*

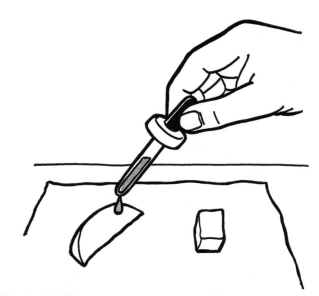

Fig. 9-4. *Test each food sample with the iodine solution.*

If the iodine turns dark brown or bluish purple, it means the food contains starch. What do the foods with starch have in common? You might have noticed that only the foods that come from plants contain starch. Throw the tested foods away when you have finished.

10

Testing for Starch in Toast

Materials

GLASS
DISH
WATER
IODINE
SLICE OF WHITE BREAD
TOASTER
TEASPOON
BUTTER KNIFE

Fill the glass about half full of water (Fig. 10-1). Add a teaspoon of iodine to the water (Fig. 10-2). Stir the solution then pour some into the dish (Fig. 10-3). Toast the bread. Now, carefully cut off a small section from the toast so that the edge is exposed to the white, untoasted center. Dip this edge into the iodine solution in the dish (Fig. 10-4). The white center of the toast will turn bluish purple indicating the presence of starch. The toasted part should not change color.

The heat from the toaster changed the starch into dextrin. The chemical makeup of dextrin is very much like that of starch. Both are carbohydrates but dextrin is easier to digest. Dextrin causes the slightly sweet taste to the crust of bread. In our bodies, dextrin forms during digestion by the action of saliva and other body fluids on starch. This is why toast is easier to digest than plain bread. Discard the food after you have finished your test.

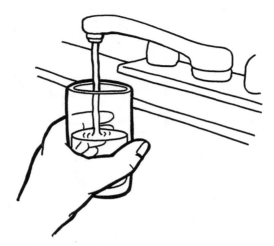

Fig. 10-1. *Pour water into the glass.*

Fig. 10-2. *Add a teaspoon of iodine.*

Fig. 10-3. *Pour the mixture into a dish.*

Fig. 10-4. *Dip a section of the bread into the solution.*

11

Testing Paper for Starch

Materials

DIFFERENT TYPES OF PAPER (NEWSPAPER, WRITING PAPER, NOTE PAPER)

SMALL GLASS

IODINE

WATER

TABLE SPOON

Put two or three tablespoons of water in the glass and add an equal amount of iodine (Fig. 11-1). Stir the solution. Dip a strip of the paper to be tested into the iodine solution (Fig. 11-2). On some of the paper, the solution will not change color, but on some of the other strips, the solution will turn bluish black or black. This indicates the presence of starch in the paper. When some papers are made, a film of a starch solution is put on it to give the paper a smooth surface and to hold the fibers together. Laundry starch works the same way on clothes. It forms a thin film that stiffens the fabric and gives it a smooth surface.

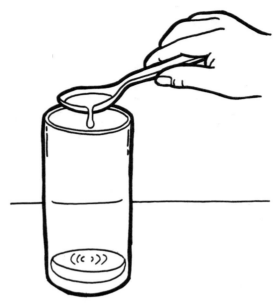

Fig. 11-1. *Put 2 or 3 tablespoons of water into the glass.*

Fig. 11-2. *Dip strips of paper into the solution to test for starch.*

12

Testing for Hard Water

Materials

DISTILLED WATER
(FROM GROCERY STORE)
TAP WATER
3 JARS WITH LIDS
MEDICINE DROPPER
BAR OF SOAP
FOOD GRATER
TABLESPOON
PENCIL, PAPER, AND TAPE

Grate a few soap flakes from the bar of soap (Fig. 12-1). Place one tablespoon of soap flakes into one of the jars, then add six tablespoons of hot water to the jar (Fig. 12-2). Mix the contents into a soapy solution and label the jar "soap."

Fill another jar about two-thirds full of tap water and label this jar "tap water." Pour the same amount of distilled water into the third jar. Place the jars side by side so that you will have equal amounts of tap water and distilled water. Label the last jar "distilled water" (Fig. 12-3).

Use the medicine dropper and add five drops of the soap solution to the jar of tap water (Fig. 12-4). Screw the lid on tight and shake the jar (Fig. 12-5). Does the soap lather? If it doesn't, add five

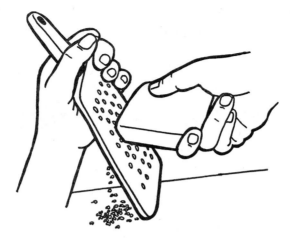

Fig. 12-1. *Grate a few flakes of soap from a bar.*

Fig. 12-2. *Add 6 tablespoons of hot water to the soap flakes.*

more drops of soap solution and shake it again. Continue adding drops of soap solution until it lathers. Count the drops to see how many it required to get it to lather.

Now, repeat the same test on the jar of distilled water. Count how many drops of soap solution it needed to get it to lather. Compare the numbers and see which type of water needed the most soap to make it lather.

The water that needed very little soap is said to be "soft water." Water that needs a lot of soap is called "hard water." In your test, the tap water should have needed more soap than the distilled water. This is because of the chemicals usually found in tap

Fig. 12-3. *Label each jar.*

Fig. 12-4. *Add 5 drops of soap solution to the tap water.*

water. The chemicals are calcium salts. The calcium in the salts reacts with the soap and makes a film. More soap must be added until all of the calcium in the water is used up, then the soap will lather. You might want to save the soap solution for other experiments.

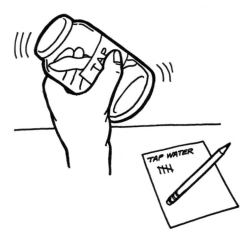

Fig. 12-5. Shake the jar to see if the soap lathers.

13

How to Make Hard Water Soft

Materials

SOAP SOLUTION
(SEE EXPERIMENT 12)
TAP WATER
WASHING SODA (NEXT TO
THE LAUNDRY DETERGENT
IN GROCERY STORE)

JAR
MEASURING SPOONS
MEDICINE DROPPER

Fill the jar with six tablespoons of tap water. Stir in one teaspoon of washing soda (Fig. 13-1). Continue to stir until the washing soda has dissolved. Now, add drops of soap solution and shake the jar (Figs. 13-2 and 13-3). Count the number of drops of soap solution it takes to get a lather. It should take much less soap to produce a lather than in the previous experiment. The washing soda has removed the hardness from the water.

Washing soda is made from sodium carbonate. The carbonate part of the soda combines with the calcium in the hard water and makes calcium carbonate. When this happens, the calcium is unable to react with the soap and the soap can lather.

Fig. 13-1. *Stir in a teaspoon of washing soda.*

Fig. 13-2. *Add drops of soap solution.*

Fig. 13-3. *Shake the jar to see if the soap lathers.*

14

How Stalactites and Stalagmites Form

Materials

2 JARS
HEAVY COTTON STRING
CARDBOARD
EPSOM SALTS (FROM GROCERY STORE)
WATER
TABLESPOON

Fill each jar about two-thirds full of water. Stir in several tablespoons of Epsom salts to each jar of water (Fig. 14-1). Keep adding salt until you have a thick solution. Now, place the jars a few inches apart on the cardboard. Lower one end of the string into one of the jars and the other end of the string into the other jar (Fig. 14-2). Let the part of the string between the jars sag to form a shallow "v."

After a few days, you will find an icicle formation growing down from the string and another growing up from the cardboard (Fig. 14-3). The one growing down is called a stalactite, and the one growing up is called a stalagmite.

Fig. 14-1. *Stir in several tablespoons of Epsom salts.*

Fig. 14-2. *Lower a string into the jars.*

Fig. 14-3. *After a few days stalactites and stalagmites will begin to form.*

In a cave, drops of water containing dissolved limestone, fall to the floor. Limestone is made of calcium carbonate and this dissolves in the water that flows over limestone rocks. Specks of calcium carbonate build up when the water evaporates. This continues year after year to make the formations.

In this experiment, the salt in the solution travels up the string and is deposited where the water drips. The salt remains after the water evaporates, creating the stalactites and stalagmites.

15

How to Make Bath Salts

Materials

SODIUM CARBONATE
COLOGNE OR PERFUME
PLASTIC BAG
ROLLING PIN OR JAR
FOOD COLORING
JAR WITH LID
TABLESPOON
2 OR 3 PAPER TOWELS
BOWL

You can buy sodium carbonate, or washing soda, from the grocery store. Put about five tablespoons of washing soda into the plastic bag (Fig. 15-1). Don't use the white, powdery lumps usually found near the top of the box. Use the clear crystals just under these. Place the paper towels, one on top of the other, on a table or counter. The towels will make a softer surface for breaking up the crystals. Put the bag of washing soda on the towels and use the rolling pin to break the crystals into smaller pieces (Fig. 15-2).

Next, empty the broken crystals into the bowl (Fig. 15-3). Add about five drops of cologne or perfume and about five drops of food coloring to the crystals (Fig. 15-4). Stir the crystals until they

Fig. 15-1. *Put about 5 tablespoons of washing soda into a plastic bag.*

Fig. 15-2. *Break the crystals into smaller pieces.*

Fig. 15-3. *Pour the broken crystals into a bowl.*

Fig. 15-4. *Add drops of cologne and food coloring to the crystals.*

are all brightly colored. Pour the crystals into the jar and put on the lid. Label the jar ''bath salts'' and keep the lid in place until you're ready to use your bath salts (Fig. 15-5).

Bath salts make hard bath water soft and the soap easier to lather. It also keeps the soap from making a film.

Fig. 15-5. Label the jar.

16

How Soap Works

Materials

JAR WITH LID

SMALL PIECE OF RAG

POWDERED LAUNDRY DETERGENT

COOKING GREASE OR SHORTENING

WATER

Fill the jar about half full of water, then add some laundry detergent and mix into a soapy solution (Fig. 16-1). Smear a small glob of grease on the rag and drop the rag into the soapy solution (Figs. 16-2 and 16-3). Replace the lid and shake the jar for a couple of minutes. Remove the rag and most, if not all, of the grease will be gone from the rag (Fig. 16-4).

Soap molecules are long. One end will dissolve in water and the other will dissolve in oil. One end of the molecule works on the particles of grease and the other end stays in the molecules of water. As more and more ends of the soap molecules try to work into the grease, they come between the grease and the cloth. They continue

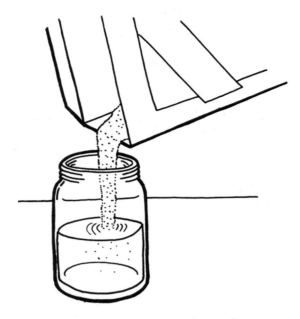

Fig. 16-1. *Add washing powder to the water.*

Fig. 16-2. *Smear grease on a rag.*

Fig. 16-3. *Put the rag into the solution and shake the jar.*

Fig. 16-4. *Most of the grease should be gone.*

to force the grease from the rag and break it up into tiny balls. Each of these tiny balls is covered with a water-liking film. This film keeps the tiny balls of grease from combining and they remain in the water when the rag is removed.

17

Soap that Eats an Egg

Materials

2 JARS
EGG (HARD-BOILED)
POWDERED LAUNDRY DETERGENT (SOME WITH ENZYMES, SOME WITHOUT)
TABLESPOON AND KNIFE
WARM WATER
PAPER, PEN, AND TAPE

Put a tablespoon of the laundry detergent containing enzymes in one of the jars and label it "enzyme." Put a tablespoon of the other laundry detergent in the other jar and label it "regular." Now put eight tablespoons of warm water in each jar (Fig. 17-1).

Have an adult help you boil an egg. When the egg is completely cooled and peeled, carefully cut two pieces of the egg white exactly the same size (Fig. 17-2) and put one piece in each jar.

Place both jars in a warm location, such as near a vent, and let them set for two days (Fig. 17-3). After two days, remove both pieces of egg white from the jars and compare their size. The one from the jar labeled enzyme should be smaller.

Fig. 17-1. *Put 8 tablespoons of warm water into each jar.*

Fig. 17-2. *Cut 2 pieces of egg white the same size.*

Fig. 17-3. *Place the jars in a warm place for two days.*

Enzyme is a proteinlike substance formed in plant and animal cells. The enzyme attacks the particles in the egg white and breaks them into smaller particles. These smaller particles then dissolve in the water. The piece of egg from the other jar should have remained the same size. This shows that the egg did not dissolve in regular laundry detergent.

Did you know we have enzymes in our stomachs? They break the food particles into small molecules that can dissolve into our blood.

18

How to Make an Acid Indicator

Materials

RED CABBAGE
TEAKETTLE AND PAN
LARGE SPOON AND KNIFE
PAPER TOWEL
FUNNEL
BOTTLE WITH A LID
WATER
STOVE
POT HOLDERS

Have an adult help you pour some water in the teakettle and heat it on the stove. While the water is heating, carefully chop up about one-fourth of the cabbage (Fig. 18-1). Place the pieces of cabbage in the pan. When the water comes to a boil, pour some over the pieces of cabbage (Fig. 18-2). Just enough to cover them. Be extremely careful—hot water can burn! Also, use pot holders because the handle will become hot. Stir the cabbage, then let the pieces soak for about 20 minutes.

Fig. 18-1. *Chop up part of a red cabbage.*

Fig. 18-2. *Cover the pieces with boiling water.*

Make a filter by folding the paper towel in half twice, then separate one of the corners to make a pocket. This shapes the paper towel into a cone. Place the funnel into the bottle and then put the cone into the funnel (Fig. 18-3). Pour the cabbage pieces and liquid into the funnel (Fig. 18-4). The paper towel filter will separate the purple-colored liquid from the cabbage. Screw on the lid and label the bottle "indicator" (Fig. 18-5). You can save this indicator solution for other experiments.

If you pour a small amount of indicator in a jar, then drop in a substance to be tested, the indicator will change color. If the indicator turns pink, the substance was an acid. If the indicator turned blue or green, the substance belonged to a group of chemicals known as alkalis. In some tests, it might take an hour or so for the indicator to change color.

Fig. 18-3. *Fold the paper towel into a filter.*

Fig. 18-4. *Pour the mixture through the filter.*

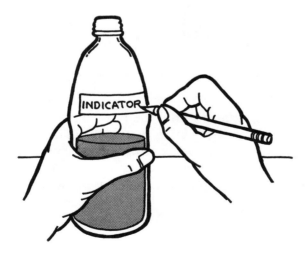

Fig. 18-5. *Label the jar.*

19

How to Make Paper Indicators

Materials

PAPERTOWEL OR PAPER
COFFEE FILTER
LIQUID INDICATOR (SEE
EXPERIMENT 18)

BOWL
BAKING PAN
SCISSORS
PLASTIC SANDWICH BAG

Pour about a cup of indicator into the bowl. Soak the paper in the bowl then place it on the pan to dry (Figs. 19-1 and 19-2). The paper should be light blue. After it has dried, cut the paper into strips about one inch wide and four inches long. The strips can be stored in the sandwich bag until ready to use (Fig. 19-3).

Fig. 19-1. *Soak the paper in the indicator.*

Fig. 19-2. *Place the paper in a pan to dry.*

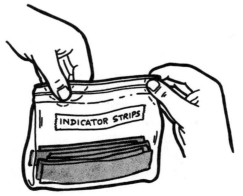

Fig. 19-3. *Cut the paper into strips. Store the strips in a sandwich bag.*

20

How to Neutralize an Acid

Materials

LEMON JUICE

BICARBONATE OF SODA (BAKING SODA)

INDICATOR (SEE EXPERIMENT 18)

MEDICINE DROPPER

TEASPOON

3 PINT-SIZED JARS

PAPER, PEN, AND TAPE

Pour about an inch of lemon juice into one of the jars and label it "acid" (Fig. 20-1). Put two, level teaspoons of baking soda in another jar. Add about one-half teaspoon of water and stir until the mixture becomes a smooth liquid. Label this jar "alkali" (Fig. 20-2). Now pour a little lemon juice acid into another jar for testing, enough to cover the bottom of the jar. Add indicator until it turns pink (Fig. 20-3). This shows that it is an acid. Next, use the medicine dropper, and add a few drops of alkali. Continue adding alkali, one drop at a time, to the acid until the pink color changes to purple. When this happens, the lemon mixture is no longer an acid. If the mixture turns green or blue, it means that too much alkali was

Fig. 20-1. *Use lemon juice for the acid.*

Fig. 20-2. *Use baking soda and water for the alkali.*

Fig. 20-3. *Add indicator to the test acid until it turns pink.*

added. Just add more acid to react with the extra alkali. When an alkali is mixed with an acid, a salt is produced. Most salts are neutral—neither acid nor basic.

Sometimes, we might have indigestion caused by too much acid in our stomachs. This can often be relieved by pills or powders made from alkalis, which neutralize our stomach acids.

21

How to Make Aluminum Shine

Materials

OLD ALUMINUM POT

(DULL)

LEMON

WATER

STOVE

KNIFE

Have an adult help you boil some water in the aluminum pot (Fig. 21-1). While the water is heating, carefully cut a couple of slices of lemon and drop them into the boiling water (Fig. 21-2). You will see the pot begin to shine.

Aluminum exposed to the air forms a thin coating of aluminum oxide. This protects the metal and keeps it from rusting, but chemicals in the water can cause discolorations after a period of time.

The citric acid from the lemon mixes with the aluminum oxide coating and forms aluminum citrate. The aluminum citrate dissolves in the boiling water and exposes the shiny metal.

Fig. 21-1. *Bring the water to a boil.*

Fig. 21-2. *Drop in a couple slices of lemon.*

22

Making Copper Shine

Materials

DULL COPPER PENNY
PAPER TOWEL
TABLE SALT
VINEGAR
MEDICINE DROPPER

Fold the paper towel in half twice and place it on a table. Place the penny on the towel and cover the penny with a thin layer of salt (Fig. 22-1). Pour a few drops of vinegar on the salt and the penny will suddenly turn bright and shiny (Fig. 22-2).

When vinegar is added to salt, the acetic acid in the vinegar mixes with the salt, or sodium chloride, and produces hydrochloric acid. This is a strong acid, and when it comes in contact with the penny, quickly removes the dull coating on the copper. Hydrochloric acid leaves the surface of the copper in a porous, active condition, and in time, the copper will corrode from combining with molecules of water, oxygen, and carbon dioxide in the air.

Fig. 22-1. *Cover the penny with a layer of salt.*

Fig. 22-2. *Add a few drops of vinegar.*

23

Flexible Bones

Materials

SEVERAL BOTTLES
OF VINEGAR

SMALL CHICKEN BONE
OR OTHER BONE

GLASS OR JAR

Put the bone in the glass and pour vinegar over the bone (Figs. 23-1 and 23-2). Add enough vinegar to completely cover the bone. Keep the bone submerged in the vinegar for about three weeks. You need to replace the old vinegar with fresh vinegar every couple of days. In about two or three weeks, remove the bone and try to bend it (Fig. 23-3). It should be flexible.

Bones are hard because they contain calcium phosphate. The acetic acid in the vinegar changed the calcium phosphate in the bone to calcium acetate. When the bone loses its calcium phosphate, it becomes flexible.

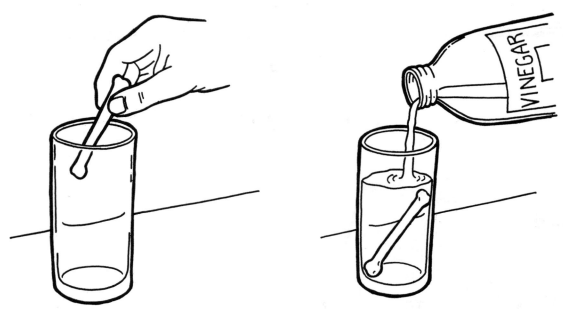

Fig. 23-1. *Put a small bone in a glass.*

Fig. 23-2. *Cover the bone with vinegar.*

Fig. 23-3. *In 2 or 3 weeks the bone will be flexible.*

24

How to Make Invisible Ink

Materials

LEMON JUICE
SMALL GLASS
TOOTHPICK
PAPER
EL'ECTRIC IRON

Pour a small amount of lemon juice into the glass (Fig. 24-1). Dip the end of the tooth pick in the lemon juice. Let the juice soak in and soften the point (Fig. 24-2). Now, write a message on the paper with the lemon juice (Fig. 24-3). You will barely be able to see it while you write, and when it dries, you can't see it at all.

Heat the iron on a high setting. Wool, for example. Place the iron on the paper and move it over the surface (Fig. 24-4). The message will soon appear. Be sure to unplug the iron when you're through and move it to a location where it can't be bumped into or knocked over, possibly burning someone.

Fig. 24-1. *Pour a little lemon juice in a glass.*

Fig. 24-2. *Soften the point of the toothpick in the juice.*

The heat from the iron burns, or chars, the lemon juice before it chars the paper. The heat causes a chemical reaction that turns the lemon juice brown. Milk can be used instead of lemon juice, but you might want to place another sheet of paper over the message to avoid damaging the surface of the iron.

Fig. 24-3. *Write a message with the juice.*

Fig. 24-4. *Heat the message to make it visible.*

25

How to Make Ink from Steel Wool

Materials

FINE STEEL WOOL
(WITHOUT SOAP)
4 TEA BAGS
WHITE VINEGAR
SMALL JAR
REGULAR CUP AND
MEASURING CUP
POT OF WATER AND A
PAN OF WATER
FAN OR HAIR DRYER

POT HOLDERS

Wash a wad of steel wool in warm soapy water to remove any oil. Dry the steel wool completely. Use a fan or hair dryer to speed the drying. Remember, using electricity near water is **very dangerous**, so be sure to dry it away from the sink. Once the steel wool is dry, place it in the jar and pour some vinegar over it (Fig. 25-1). The steel wool should be completely covered with vinegar.

Place the jar in a pan of water on the stove (Fig. 25-2). Heat the water but not to the boiling point. Next, put about a half cup of water and the four tea bags in the pot and heat it to the boiling point (Fig. 25-3). Now allow both solutions to cool.

Fig. 25-1. *Cover the steel wool with vinegar.*

Fig. 25-2. *Heat the jar in a pan of water.*

Fig. 25-3. *Add four tea bags to about a half cup of water.*

Fig. 25-4. *Pour an equal amount of each solution into a cup and stir.*

Pour an equal amount of each solution into the cup and stir (Fig. 25-4). The solution should be almost colorless. Dip a small paint brush, or your finger, into the solution and make a mark on a piece of paper (Fig. 25-5). As the mark dries, it will change color. In time, three to five hours, it should be ink black.

Fig. 25-5. *Use a small brush to make a mark.*

The reaction between the iron in the steel wool and the vinegar produced iron acetate and hydrogen. The tea in the boiling water produced tannin. When the two solutions were mixed in the cup, they produced iron tannate. This turns into an iron-tannate complex that changes form and color as it comes in contact with the air and dries.

Experiment

26

How to Grow Sugar Crystals

Materials

- PENCIL
- STRING (ABOUT 6 INCHES LONG)
- SMALL WEIGHT
- THIN CARDBOARD
- GLASS OR JAR
- TABLESPOON
- SUGAR
- WATER

Fill the glass about three-fourths full of water (Fig. 26-1). Stir in several tablespoons of sugar (Fig. 26-2). Keep adding sugar until the solution becomes saturated. This is the point where the water will accept no more sugar. Stir until all of the sugar is dissolved. Now, tie one end of the string around the pencil and the other end to the weight (Fig. 26-3). Make a slit in the cardboard then slide the string through the slit and lower the weight into the solution (Fig. 26-4). Suspend the weight just above the bottom of the glass. The weight is used just to keep the string straight. The cardboard should cover the glass and the pencil should rest on the cardboard. The cardboard is used to slow the rate of evaporation. Put the glass in a

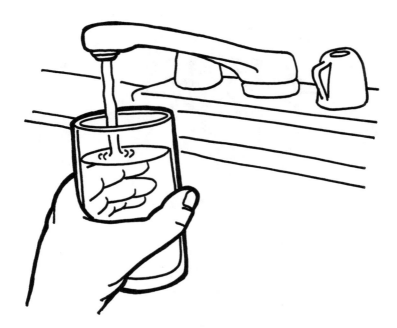

Fig. 26-1. *Fill the glass with water.*

Fig. 26-2. *Stir in several tablespoons of sugar.*

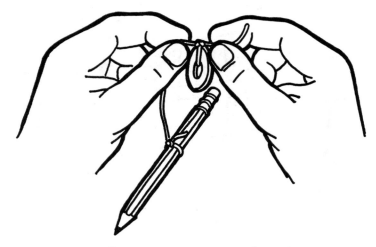

Fig. 26-3. *Attach a weight to the string.*

Fig. 26-4. *Lower the string into the solution.*

dry place and let the solution stand for at least three weeks. This will give it time for the crystal to form (Fig. 26-5).

If the solution is allowed to evaporate too fast, the sugar molecules will form crystals wherever they happen to be. When the evaporation rate is slower, the sugar molecules will join together to form larger crystals. The slower the evaporation, the larger the crystals.

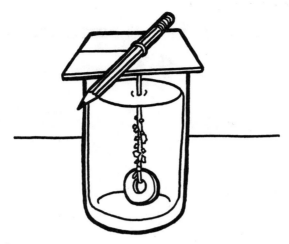

Fig. 26-5. *In about three weeks, crystals will begin to form.*

27

How to Grow a Crystal Garden

Materials

BROKEN PIECES OF
BRICK OR COAL

PAN

PINT JAR

TABLESPOON

SALT

WATER

Fill the jar half full of water. Stir in several tablespoons of salt (Fig. 27-1). Keep adding salt until the water is saturated. This is when no more salt can be dissolved in the water. Place the pieces of brick in the pan and pour some of the salt solution over the pieces (Figs. 27-2 and 27-3). Let the solution stand and in a day or so you should see crystals growing on the surfaces of the pieces of brick (Fig. 27-4).

The crystals form because the saltwater moves up through the tiny openings in the brick by capillary action. This is when the liquid wets the brick inside the tiny openings and draws itself up

Fig. 27-1. Stir several tablespoons of salt into the water.

Fig. 27-2. Place a piece of broken brick in the pan.

like a paper towel absorbing water. When the water reaches the air, it begins to evaporate leaving the salt. As the water evaporates, the molecules in the salt start to cling together and grow into larger crystals.

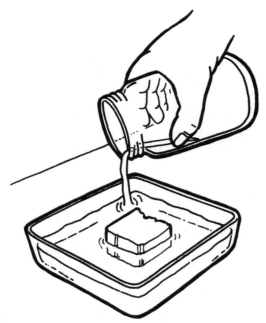

Fig. 27-3. *Pour some of the salt solution over the piece of brick.*

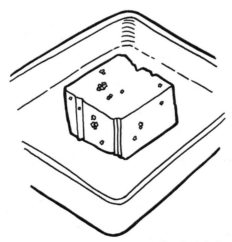

Fig. 27-4. *Crystals will begin to grow on the brick in a couple of days.*

28

How to Make Carbon Dioxide

Materials

BAKING SODA
VINEGAR
JAR
TEASPOON

Pour enough vinegar into the jar to cover the bottom about one-fourth inch (Fig. 28-1). Add a few teaspoons of baking soda to the vinegar (Fig. 28-2). The mixture will quickly begin to fizz and bubble. It is generating carbon dioxide gas, and as the gas escapes, it makes the mixture bubble.

Fig. 28-1. *Pour vinegar into a jar.*

Fig. 28-2. *Add a little baking soda to the vinegar.*

29

Carbon Dioxide and Fire

Materials

CANDLE AND MATCHES
VINEGAR
BAKING SODA
LARGE, WIDE-MOUTH JAR
PROTECTIVE GLOVES

Stand the candle upright in the bottom of the jar (Fig. 29-1). Pour vinegar into the jar (Fig. 29-2). Just enough to cover the bottom of the jar. Carefully light the candle (Fig. 29-3). After the candle has established a good flame, add a little baking soda to the vinegar in the bottom of the jar (Fig. 29-4). The mixture will start to bubble and the flame will soon go out (Fig. 29-5). The candle needs oxygen for it to burn. The carbon dioxide pushes away the oxygen and suffocates the flame.

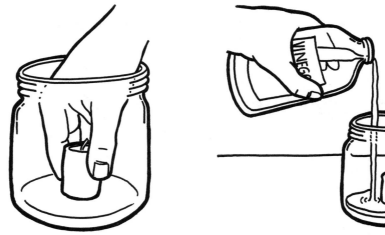

Fig. 29-1. *Place a candle in the jar.*

Fig. 29-2. *Add a little vinegar.*

Fig. 29-3. *Carefully light the candle.*

Fig. 29-4. *Add baking soda to the vinegar.*

Fig. 29-5. *Carbon dioxide gas puts out the flame.*

30

Testing For Carbon Dioxide

Materials

BAKING SODA AND VINEGAR

CLEAR PLASTIC BOTTLE WITH PLASTIC LID (ASPIRIN BOTTLE)

LARGE NAIL

MODELING CLAY

FLEXIBLE, PLASTIC TUBING (ABOUT ¼ INCH IN DIAMETER AND 18 INCHES LONG) FROM HARDWARE STORE

LIME FROM GARDEN SUPPLY STORE (GARDEN LIME OR HYDRATED LIME MADE FROM CALCIUM HYDROXIDE NOT THE KIND MADE FROM CALCIUM CARBONATE OR CALCIUM OXIDE)

3 JARS WITH LIDS

TEASPOON

WATER

PAPER, PEN, AND TAPE

For this experiment, you will need something to generate the gas and some limewater to test the gas.

Use the nail to make a hole in the lid of the plastic bottle. Make it just large enough for the tubing to fit through. Now push one end of the tube into this hole (Fig. 30-1). Let it stick through about one-fourth inch. Press the clay around the tube and the hole to make a seal (Fig. 30-2).

To make the limewater, put about three teaspoons of lime in the jar and fill it about half full of water (Fig. 30-3). Stir the mixture and then allow it to settle for three or four hours, or until the solution is clear. Then pour the clear part of the liquid into another jar and label it "limewater" (Fig. 30-4).

90

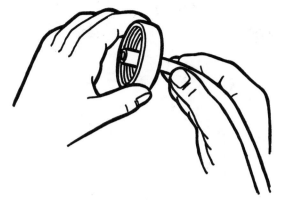

Fig. 30-1. *Push one end of the tube through the hole.*

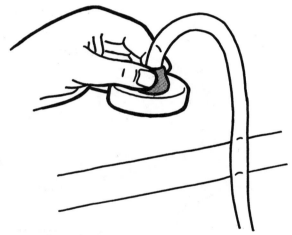

Fig. 30-2. *Seal the lid with modeling clay.*

Fig. 30-3. *Stir 3 teaspoons of lime into the water.*

Fig. 30-4. *Pour the clear limewater into a jar.*

To perform the test, pour about an inch of limewater into a jar and fill the plastic bottle about one-third full of vinegar (Fig. 30-5). Now, working quickly, add three or four teaspoons of baking soda to the vinegar and put on the lid (Fig. 30-6). Lower the free end of the tube into the limewater (Fig. 30-7). The limewater should begin to bubble and might continue to bubble for a couple of minutes. Notice the change in the limewater. It should become cloudy.

Limewater will turn cloudy when carbon dioxide gas is bubbled through it. This means that when baking soda is added to vinegar, it will produce carbon dioxide gas.

You can save the unused limewater and plastic bottle and tubing for other experiments. To make more limewater, just add water to the lime that remained in the mixing jar and let it settle as before. Keep a lid on the limewater until you are ready to use it again.

Fig. 30-5. *Pour vinegar into the plastic jar.*

Fig. 30-6. *Add baking soda to the vinegar and replace the lid.*

Fig. 30-7. *The limewater should become cloudy.*

31

Testing Your Breath for Carbon Dioxide

Materials

JAR

LIMEWATER (SEE EXPERIMENT 30)

DRINKING STRAW

Pour a little limewater in the jar (Fig. 31-1) and use the straw to blow your breath through the limewater (Fig. 31-2). Be careful not to suck any of the limewater into your mouth. You might have to blow for two or three minutes, but then the limewater should turn cloudy. This means that our breath contains carbon dioxide.

Fig. 31-1. *Pour limewater into the jar.*

Fig. 31-2. *The limewater should become cloudy.*

32

Identifying Unknown Ingredients

Materials

LIQUID INDICATOR
(SEE EXPERIMENT 18)
FLOUR, POWDERED
SUGAR, BAKING SODA,
SALT, AND CREAM OF
TARTAR
5 JARS AND 5 CUPS
TEASPOON
WARM WATER
VINEGAR

PEN, PAPER, AND TAPE

Put two teaspoons of flour into one of the jars. Clean the spoon, then put two teaspoons of powdered sugar into another jar. Continue cleaning the spoon and putting two teaspoons of each ingredient into separate jars. Now, move the jars around until you can't remember which jar contains what ingredient. Label each jar with a number one through five and do the same to the cups (Fig. 32-1). Always test the same number ingredient in the same cup. Powder 1 in cup 1, powder 2 in cup 2, and so on.

Begin the test by finding out if any of the powders are neutral, an acid, or alkaline. Pour a small amount of indicator into each of the test cups (Fig. 32-2), then add a bit of powder 1 to cup 1, powder 2 to cup 2, and so on. Watch for a change in color of the indicator in the test cup. If the indicator turned pink, the powder was an acid. If it turned blue or green, the powder was alkaline. Cream of tartar is an acid. Most salts are neutral and baking soda is alkaline. Flour and sugar are neutral. Make a chart to record the tests for each numbered ingredient (Fig. 32-3). For example, number two might be an acid while number one and four might be alkaline.

Now, wash each test cup and put two teaspoons of each powder into separate cups again. This time, add about a half of a cup warm water to each powder and stir to see if it dissolves. Four of the powders should dissolve. Flour is the only one that should not dissolve. This is because flour is made up of tiny particles of grain, such as wheat, while sugar, salt, baking soda, and cream of tartar are made up of chemical compounds. Record the results on your chart.

Fig. 32-1. *Label the unknown ingredients with numbers.*

Fig. 32-2. *Use indicator to test for acids and alkalis.*

Fig. 32-3. *Make a chart and record the tests.*

Next, use the plastic bottle and tubing (see Experiment 30) to test each powder to see if it makes carbon dioxide (Fig. 32-4). Add a little vinegar to each powder and use the indicator. If it turns cloudy, the powder should be baking soda. Record these results on the chart. With the information you have gathered, you will be able to identify each of the five powders.

Fig. 32-4. *Test each powder to see if it makes carbon dioxide.*

33

How to Separate Water

Materials

9-VOLT BATTERY

2 PENCIL LEADS (FROM MECHANICAL PENCIL) OR 2 PENCILS SHARPENED ON BOTH ENDS

2 FLEXIBLE COPPER WIRES (ABOUT 18 INCHES LONG)

2 SMALL PAPER CLIPS

SCISSORS AND TAPE

CLEAR GLASS OR JAR

TAP WATER

Carefully trim about one inch of the insulation from each end of the wires with the scissors (Fig. 33-1). Connect the end of one of the wires to one of the terminals of the battery (Fig. 33-2). You can form a loop and twist the bare end around the terminal. Tape will help hold it in place. Connect the other bare end of the wire to one of the paper clips (Fig. 33-3). Make the connections tight.

Connect the bare end of the other wire to the other terminal of the battery. Connect the other end of the wire to the other paper clip, like the first wire. Next, clamp a paper clip to the end of one of the pieces of pencil lead. Clamp the other paper clip to the other pencil lead.

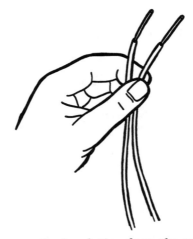

Fig. 33-1. *Remove the insulation from the ends of the wires.*

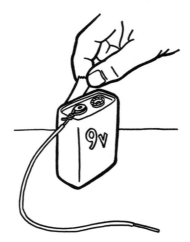

Fig. 33-2. *Use tape to hold the wires in place.*

Fig. 33-3. *Attach the paper clip to the pencil lead.*

Fill the glass nearly to the top with water. Position each paper clip on the rim of the glass so that both pencil leads extend down into the water (Fig. 33-4). Notice the bubbles forming on the pencil leads. You will see that one has more bubbles than the other. About twice as many. One is creating oxygen bubbles and the other is making bubbles of hydrogen.

The water in the glass is completing an electrical circuit. An electrical current flows from the battery, down through the pencil lead, through the water, to the other pencil lead and back to the battery. The water, and everything, is made up of tiny particles called atoms. These atoms cling together and form molecules. Each water molecule is made up of one oxygen atom and two hydrogen atoms. When the electrical current flowed from the battery, the water molecules separated into atoms of oxygen and hydrogen. Water has twice as many hydrogen atoms than oxygen atoms, so twice as many hydrogen bubbles formed than oxygen bubbles.

Fig. 33-4. *Bubbles of oxygen and hydrogen will form.*

34

How to Make Oxygen

Materials

CLEAR PLASTIC JAR
WITH LID (SUCH AS A
PEANUT BUTTER JAR)
FLEXIBLE PLASTIC
TUBING
ACTIVATED CHARCOAL
(FROM AQUARIUM
SUPPLIES)
HYDROGEN PEROXIDE
(FROM THE DRUG STORE)

BOARD
LARGE NAIL
HAMMER
TEST TUBE
WOODEN MATCH
MODELING CLAY
LARGE, DEEP PAN
SAFETY GOGGLES
PROTECTIVE GLOVES

With your safety goggles on, use a board, a nail and a hammer to carefully punch a hole in the plastic lid. You must make the hole just large enough for the tubing to fit through. As shown in Fig. 34-1, push one end of the tubing through the hole about one-fourth inch. Make a seal by pressing modeling clay around the tube and the hole (Fig. 34-2).

Put about one inch of activated charcoal in the plastic jar. Now fill the large pan and the test tube with water. Put the test tube—turned upside down—in the water (Fig. 34-3). You can do this by putting your thumb over the mouth of the test tube before turning the tube upside down. While keeping the mouth of the test tube

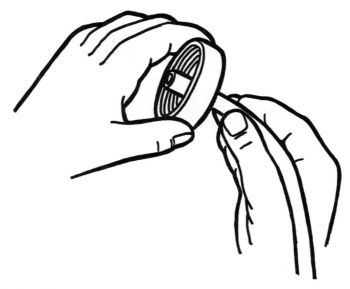

Fig. 34-1. *Push one end of the tubing through the hole.*

under water, put the free end of the flexible tubing into the test tube until it reaches the bottom of the test tube.

The next step must be done quickly. The reaction is very fast. Fill the plastic jar about one-half full with hydrogen peroxide, and attach the lid. As the chemical reaction takes place, the level of the water in the test tube should decrease. The water in the test tube is being replaced with a gas.

To test the gas, carefully remove the test tube from the large pan of water. If any water remains in the test tube, tip the mouth of the tube slightly to allow the water to escape. Next, while wearing safety gloves, insert a glowing match—not a full flame—into the test tube. If the match bursts into flames, then the gas you produced was oxygen.

Hydrogen peroxide (H_2O_2) contains some oxygen that is not very stable. When the peroxide comes into contact with the activated charcoal, a chemical reaction occurs to release oxygen gas and water. The charcoal does not chemically react. However, it is needed for this reaction to take place. When a material is needed to force a chemical reaction to happen, it is called a catalyst.

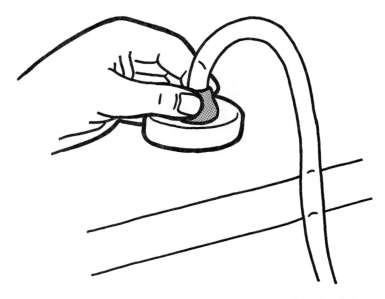

Fig. 34-2. *Use modeling clay to make a seal in the lid.*

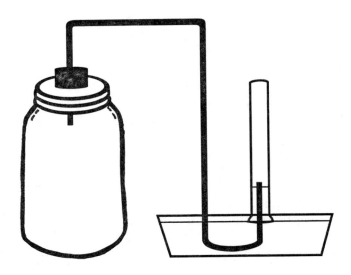

Fig. 34-3. *Fill the pan and test tube with water. Put about one inch of activated charcoal in the plastic jar.*

35

Rusting Iron and Oxygen

Materials

STEEL WOOL
TALL, NARROW JAR
(OLIVE JAR) OR TEST
TUBE
BOWL
WATER
WOODEN MATCH

Wash the steel wool in soap and warm water to remove any oil. Wet the inside of the jar and place a small wad of the steel wool inside (Fig. 35-1). Fill the bowl with about two inches of water. Now, place the jar upside down in the bowl of water (Fig. 35-2). Let the experiment set a couple of days. The steel wool will begin to rust and the water level in the jar will rise. Place your hand over the opening of the jar to trap the air inside, as you lift the jar from the bowl of water and turn it right side up. Light the match and remove your hand from the mouth of the jar (Fig. 35-3). Now, quickly put the flame down into the air in the jar. The flame should go out (Fig. 35-4).

Fig. 35-1. *Place a small wad of steel wool inside the jar.*

Fig. 35-2. *Turn the jar upside down and place it in the water.*

When something burns, like the match, one or more substances in the match combine with oxygen and give off heat and light. But when some substances combine with oxygen, they do not get hot and give off light. Rusting iron is an example.

When just one other element is combined with oxygen, it is called an oxide. The oxygen in the air in the jar combined with the element iron in the steel wool and formed iron oxide, or rust. The water level in the jar rose as some of the oxygen in the jar was consumed. The lack of oxygen is what put the match out.

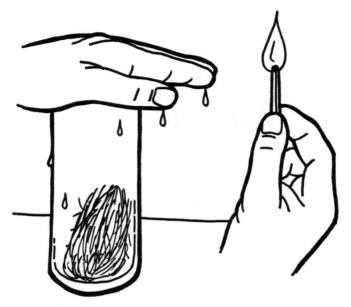

Fig. 35-3. *Remove the jar from the water.*

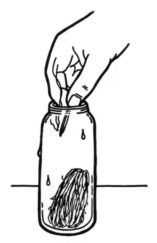

Fig. 35-4. *The flame should go out.*

36
Quick Rust

Materials

2 NAILS
9 VOLT CALCULATOR
BATTERY
2 PIECES OF
COPPER WIRE
SMALL GLASS
SALT
WARM WATER
TABLESPOON
SCISSORS

Fill the glass with about two inches of warm water and stir in a couple of tablespoons of salt (Fig. 36-1). Strip a couple of inches of the insulation from the ends of both wires with the scissors. Twist one of the ends of one wire tightly around one of the nails near the head (Fig. 36-2). Wrap the other end of this wire around one of the terminals of the battery. Now, twist one of the ends of the other wire around the other nail and connect the other end to the remaining terminal of the battery (Fig. 36-3).

Lower the nails into the salty solution, keeping them separated from each other (Fig. 36-4). Bubbles will immediately start forming around one of the nails and not around the other. After a few minutes, remove the nails and examine them (Fig. 36-5). The nail

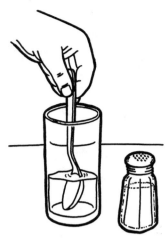

Fig. 36-1. *Stir salt into some warm water.*

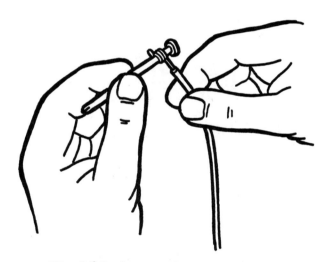

Fig. 36-2. *Connect the wire to the nail.*

connected to the negative terminal of the battery will still be shiny, while the one connected to the positive terminal will have started to rust.

The shiny nail had a negative polarity. This attracted the hydrogen in the solution and formed the bubbles. The hydrogen bubbles kept the nail from oxidation. The nail connected to the positive terminal attracted chlorine from the solution and this attacks the nail and causes rapid corrosion, or rust.

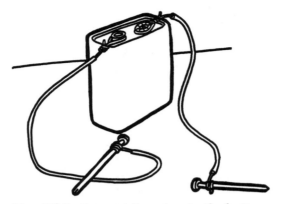

Fig. 36-3. Connect the wires to the battery.

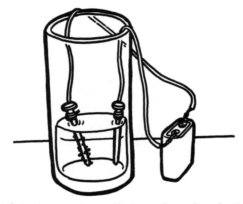

Fig. 36-4. Lower the nails into the salt solution.

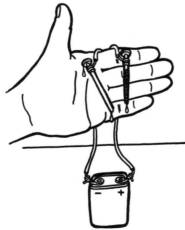

Fig. 36-5. The nail connected to the positive terminal will have started to rust.

37
Oxygen and Fire

Materials

SMALL CANDLE
MATCHES
METAL LID FROM
POP BOTTLE
JAR
PROTECTIVE GLOVES

Over a kitchen counter or tabletop, light the candle and melt a little wax in the lid (Fig. 37-1). Wear protective gloves. Now, stand the candle in the melted wax (Fig. 37-2). This will be a base for the candle. Turn the jar upside down and cover the burning candle (Fig. 37-3). Soon the flame will go out.

The flame needs oxygen to burn. When the jar was placed over the candle, the flame consumed most of the oxygen in the jar and the flame went out.

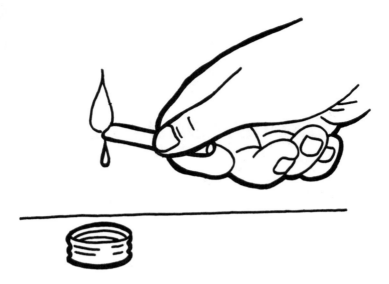

Fig. 37-1. *Drop melted wax into the lid.*

Fig. 37-2. *Place the jar over the candle.*

Fig. 37-3. *The flame will go out.*

38

Carbon in a Flame

Materials

CANDLE AND MATCHES
(FROM EXPERIMENT 7)
METAL PAN OR LID
PROTECTIVE GLOVES

Over a kitchen countertop or tabletop, light the candle and notice how the flame burns (Fig. 38-1). As the flame burns, it produces moisture and carbon, along with other substances. Wear protective gloves and be sure to hold the candle at an angle so that the hot does not drip on your hands. Now hold the piece of metal in the flame (Fig. 38-2). You will soon see a coating of black soot on the metal (Fig. 38-3). This is carbon.

When the candle is allowed to burn freely, the carbon mixes with the oxygen in the air and produces carbon dioxide. But when

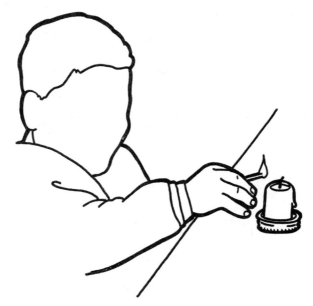

Fig. 38-1. *Light the candle.*

Fig. 38-2. *Hold the metal in the flame.*

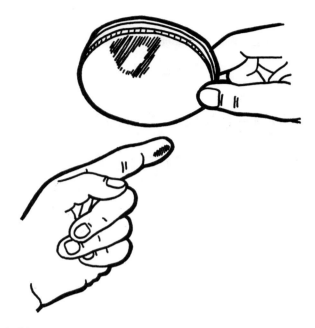

Fig. 38-3. *Unburned carbon is deposited on the metal.*

the metal was held in the flame, it lowered the temperature of the flame. The carbon could not mix with the oxygen at this lower temperature. This caused the unburned carbon to be deposited on the metal in the form of soot.

39

Baking Soda
Fire Extinguisher

Materials

BAKING SODA
SMALL CANDLE
METAL LID OR PAN

Place the candle in the lid and carefully light the candle (Fig. 39-1). Let it burn a few seconds so that the flame is well developed. At this point, sprinkle baking soda over the flame, and it will quickly be extinguished (Fig. 39-2). Baking soda is a very good material for putting out grease fires.

As the baking soda is heated, it breaks up into three parts: sodium carbonate, water, and carbon dioxide. The sodium carbonate forms a coating on the grease. This helps put out the fire. The water lowers the temperature, and this helps put out the fire. And the carbon dioxide cuts off the supply of oxygen to the fire. Without oxygen, the fire can't burn.

Fig. 39-1. *Light the candle and let it burn a few moments.*

Fig. 39-2. *Sprinkle baking soda over the flame.*

PART II

SCIENCE FAIRS

A well-chosen science fair project can be exciting and educational. The important term here is "well chosen." Spend some time just thinking about a subject (Fig. 1). This planning stage might be the most important part of the project. Use your imagination, but don't pick something too difficult or too complicated.

Begin your planning by breaking your project down into four steps:

1. Selecting a topic.

2. Questions and hypothesis. A hypothesis is just your guess of what you think the outcome of the experiment will be.

3. Doing the experiment.

4. The results and conclusions of your experiment.

Fig. 1. Give your project a lot of thought.

You probably will want to make a report on your experiment. This should show the purpose of the experiment and answer a question or prove a hypothesis. Your report should include the experiment itself, the results of the experiment, and the conclusions that you made. Graphs and charts are often useful in displaying information in a clear and simple form.

When choosing your topic, pick something you are really interested in, or want to learn about. Something you can get excited about. Avoid experiments that are too complicated or that require materials that are expensive or hard to get. Try to choose an experiment that you can complete with the materials and equipment you have available or that you can build. Many of the greatest scientific discoveries were based on a simple principle.

After selecting a topic, break it down to a specific problem to solve or a question to be answered. For example, the subject of corrosion could be narrowed down to showing how a variety of different coatings prevent oxidation, or rust. You could compare the materials to prove which one was the best and which one was the most economical. Or, you could try to discover a better material than salt to melt ice on streets. Where this practice is in use, it causes extensive corrosion to the lower part of vehicles.

The experiment on testing unknown chemicals could be used to test your local drinking water for the chemicals it contains (Fig. 2). Tap water is not pure. Chemicals from the rocks in the ground dissolve and get into the water supply. Sometimes, even chemicals from agricultural operations or manufacturing plants filter down through the soil and pollute water supplies. Water companies are constantly analyzing water to ensure clean water.

You might want to examine the foods found in the home for acids (Fig. 3). You can easily demonstrate this by performing acid tests on foods such as baking soda, cola, tea, vinegar, and milk.

Suppose you're interested in the experiment about separating water (Fig. 4). This could lead to an experiment on the possibilities of hydrogen as a clean-burning, inexpensive fuel. This would probably be too difficult to construct a working example, but you could show that it can be done and give examples of how hydrogen could be used.

After you have selected a topic and decided on a project, think about the materials you are going to need. You might want to build a model. Models can usually be built out of wood or cardboard. Don't overlook normal household throwaways such as empty jars, cardboard tubes from paper towels, and empty coffee cans (Fig. 5).

Fig. 2. *You can test your drinking water for chemicals.*

Fig. 3. *Foods can be tested for acids.*

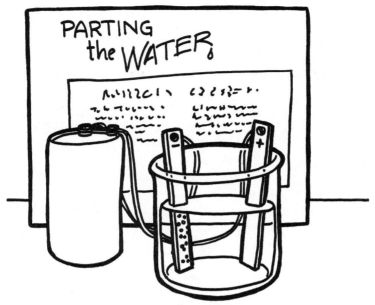

Fig. 4. *You can separate hydrogen from water.*

Fig. 5. *Household throwaways can often be used in experiments.*

Be creative. Use your imagination.

You will probably be able to display your experiment on a table. A self-supporting panel made from heavy cardboard and slightly bent to form three sections can stand behind your experiment. It would look something like a miniature theater stage (Fig. 6).

The left section of the panel could show the purpose of your experiment. The section in the middle could contain drawings of the experiment and the right section could show the results and conclusions of your experiment.

Try to be creative. Develop your own ideas. Use the experiments you find in books to help you work out your own ideas. Your experiment doesn't have to be original, just try it from a different point of view. Most experiments have been done before, but yours might be improved or put to a better use.

Fig. 6. *The panel can display information about your experiment.*

Keep good notes of your experiment. Always write down quantities, times, or other conditions that might be important to understanding the results of your experiment. You will also need this information to put your notes together for your display and your conclusions.

Do some research at your school or neighborhood library on the topic you've decided to do an experiment on. This way, you'll find out what's already been done, or maybe try to solve a problem.

Finally, have fun with your experiment and don't be afraid to try new and different things. Science principles are always changing because someone discovered a new method for doing something or a new way to use a scientific proof, and *that's* exciting.

Glossary

acid   A compound that can react with a base to form a salt.

alkali   Any soluble mineral salt, or mixture of salts, found in soil and capable of neutralizing acids.

alloys   A mixture of two or more metals.

atom   Any of the smallest particles of an element that combine with similar particles of other elements to produce compounds.

base   A substance which forms a salt when it reacts with an acid.

capillary action   The movement, caused by surface tension and other forces, of a liquid through tiny openings in a solid.

carbohydrates   Certain organic compounds, including sugar, starch and celluloses. They make up an important class of food in animal nutrition, supplying energy to the body.

compound   A material made up of two or more elements joined together.

contract   Shrink in size.

corrosion   The eating or wearing away gradually as by rusting or by the action of chemicals.

distilled   Something that has been refined or made more nearly pure by first heating and then allowing to cool and condense.

element   A material made up of only one kind of atom.

enzyme A proteinlike substance found in plants and animals that speeds up specific chemical reactions.

evaporate To change a liquid into a vapor.

hypothesis A guess used by scientists to explain how or why something happens.

molecules The smallest particle of an element or compound that can exist in the free state and still retain the characteristics of the element or compound.

neutral A state in which a substance is neither acid nor alkali.

oxidation Chemical change combining oxygen with another substance.

oxide Any compound that is made up of oxygen combined with one other element.

polarity The condition of being positive or negative with respect to some reference point.

saturated Having absorbed all that can be taken up.

soluble Something that can be dissolved or made into a solution.

solution A mixture of dissolved materials.

starch A white tasteless, odorless food substance found in many vegetables.

tincture of iodine A diluted solution of iodine.

volume A space occupied by matter.

Index

A

acids
    aluminum polished with, 65-66
    base plus, salts from, 16-17
    copper polished with, 67-68
    indicator for, 56-59
    indicators for, paper-strip, 60-61
    invisible ink, 71-73
    neutralization of, 62-64
    softening bones with, 69-70
    testing foods for, 123-124
    testing for, 97-100
alchemy, viii
alcohol, molecule size, 6-9
alkalis (*see also* bases)
    acid neutralized with, 62-64
    testing for, 97-100
alloys, viii
aluminum, viii
    acids to polish, 65-66

B

baking soda extinguisher, 118-119
bases (*see also* alkalis)
    acids plus, salts from, 16-17
bath salts, 45-48
bones, acid softening of, 69-70

C

cadmium, viii
capillary action, 82
carbon, viii
    flames producing, 115-117
carbon dioxide
    fire vs., 87-89
    making, 85-86
    testing for, 90-94
    testing for, breath, 95-96

charts, 123
chemistry, vii
chlorine, viii
compounds, viii
conclusions, 122
copper, viii
    acid to polish, 67-68
crystal garden, 82-84
crystals
    salts, 82-84
    sugar, 78-81

D

displays, 126
distillation, 35

E

elements, viii
energy, vii
enzymes, 53-55
expansion, gases, 24-26
experiments, 122-123, 125-127

F

fire
    baking soda extinguisher,
      118-119
    carbon dioxide vs., 87-89
    carbon from, 115-117
    oxygen and, 113-114
formulas, viii

G

gases
    expansion of, 24-26

heat's effect on, 21-23
gold, viii
graphs, 123

H

hard water
    softening, 39-41
    testing, 35-38
heat
    chemical changes from, 18-20,
      30-32
    solids and gases, 21-23
hydrogen, viii
    fuel from, 123
    separating water for, 101-103
hypothesis, 122-123

I

ice, melting point of, salt vs.,
    10-12
ink
    invisible, 71-73
    steel wool for, 74-77
invisible ink, 71-73
iron, viii
    oxygen, rust and, 107-109

L

limestone, 42-44

M

magnesium, viii
medicines, vii-viii
melting point
    chemical changes at, 18-20
    salt and ice, 10-12
metals, viii
models, 123, 126
molecules, size of, water vs.
    alcohol, 6-9

N

note-taking, 127

O

oxygen, viii
    fire and, 113-114
    making, 104-106
    rusting iron and, 107-109
    separating water for, 101-103

P

plastics, viii

R

reports, 123
research, 127
results, 122
rust, quick, 110-112

S

safety precautions, ix
salt (sodium-chloride), viii
    crystals, 82-84
    melting point of ice and, 10-12
    volume of salt water, 3-5
salts, viii
    bath salts, 45-48
    making, 16-17
    softening hard water with,
      39-41
soap
    chemical action of, 49-52
    egg-eating enzymes, 53-55
sodium, viii
sodium carbonate, 39
softening hard water, 39-41
solids, heat's effect on, 21-23
solubility, 13-15
stalactites, 42-44
stalagmites, 42-44
starches
    sugar formed from, 30-32
    testing for, 27-29
    testing for, paper, 33-34
    testing for, toast, 30-32
steel wool, ink from, 74-77
sugar crystals, 78-81
symbols for elements, viii

T

tannin, 77
testing for unknown ingredients,
    97-100
topic selection, 122-123

V

volume, salt water, 3-5

W

water
    hard, softening, 39-41
    hard, testing for, 35-38
    iodine removed from, 13-15
    molecule size, 6-9
    separating into hydrogen and
        oxygen, 101-103, 123, 125
    testing for chemicals, 123-124

Other Bestsellers of Related Interest

Botany: 49 More Science Fair Projects
—Robert L. Bonnet and G. Daniel Keen
Encourages the development of reasoning skills essential to all scientific inquiry. Throughout, the authors stress the importance of control groups and accurate record-keeping as the basis for scientific discovery. Numerous illustrations and tables help students to record data and to keep their projects organized. Guidelines for judging science fair projects, a complete glossary of botanical terms, and a listing of lab equipment and hydroponic supply sources round out the volume.
0-8306-3416-9, #156666-X $10.95 Paper

How? More Experiments for the Young Scientist
—Dave Prochnow and Kathy Prochnow
Provides more than 40 illustrated experiments in astronomy, aerodynamics, engineering, life sciences, chemistry, meteorology, and physics—for children ages 8–13. Each a self-contained lesson on focusing on a specific natural or man-made occurrence, these projects teach children important learning skills like following directions, observing carefully, and accurately recording information.
0-8306-4025-8, #051052-0 $10.95 Paper

Insect Biology: 49 Science Fair Projects
—H. Steven Dashefsky
Here is a rich source of experimentation in one of the most accessible and fascinating fields of science, with more than 40 complete, step-by-step science fair projects for children ages 8 to 13. Experiments teach the role of insects in ecosystems; basic invertebrate anatomy and physiology; the remarkable diversity of insect life; and phenomena such as phototropism, altruism, and adaptive coloration.
0-8306-4032-0, #015658-1 $10.95 Paper
0-8306-4031-2, #015657-3 $18.95 Hard

Physics for Kids: 49 Easy Experiments in Electricity and Magnetism
—*Robert W. Wood*

These projects highlight the relationship between electricity and magnetism, the difference between current and static electricity, and how negative and positive changes occur.

0-8306-3412-6, #156616-3 $10.95 Paper

Science for Kids: 39 Easy Astronomy Experiments
—*Robert W. Wood*

Acquaints young experimenters ages 8 through 13 with the study of heavenly bodies and their motion through experiments and projects such as making maps of the stars and constellations and building a sundial.

0-8306-3597-1, #156195-1 $10.95 Paper

Science for Kids: 39 Easy Geography Activities
—*Robert W. Wood*

Designed to teach children geography skills while sparking an interest in world cultures, anthropology, and current events, this book includes illustrated projects that involve the use of maps and globes.

0-8306-2492-9, #157869-2 $10.95 Paper

Science for Kids: 39 Easy Meteorology Experiments
—*Robert W. Wood*

Introduces students to the fascinating field of meteorology through experiments that will help them understand the principles of air pressure, cold and warm fronts, clouds, and other forces that make up weather.

0-8306-3595-5, #071723-0 $10.95 Paper
0-8306-6595-1, #071722-2 $16.95 Hard

Science for Kids: 39 Easy Plant Biology Experiments
—*Robert W. Wood*

Introduces readers ages 8 through 13 to the study and use of plants for food, medicine, and manufacturing, complete with fully illustrated, entertaining, and education experiments.

0-8306-1935-6, #071728-1 $10.95 Paper
0-8306-1941-0, #071729-X $16.95 Hard

Science for Kids: 39 Engineering Experiments
—Robert W. Wood
Introduces students ages 8 through 13 to the principles that guide engineers in the design of aircraft, cars, skyscrapers, highways, bridges, and more.
0-8306-1943-7, #071740-0 $10.95 Paper

Environmental Science: 49 Science Fair Projects
—Robert L. Bonnet/G. Daniel Keen
Introduces young experimenters to the fundamental workings of their natural surroundings while raising their awareness of pollution, water contamination, and environmentally stressed wildlife.
0-8306-3369-3, #156104-8 $10.95 Paper
0-8306-7369-5, #156094-7 $17.95 Hard

EASY ORDER FORM— SATISFACTION GUARANTEED

How to Order

 Call 1-800-822-8158
24 hours a day,
7 days a week
in U.S. and Canada

 Mail this coupon to:
McGraw-Hill, Inc.
P.O. Box 182067
Columbus, OH 43218-2607

 Fax your order to:
614-759-3644

 EMAIL
70007.1531@COMPUSERVE.COM
COMPUSERVE: GO MH

Ship to:
Name _____
Address _____
City/State/Zip _____
Daytime Telephone No. _____

Thank you for your order!

ITEM NO.	QUANTITY	AMT.

Method of Payment:
☐ Check or money order enclosed (payable to McGraw-Hill)
☐ DISCOVER
☐ AMERICAN EXPRESS Cards
☐ VISA
☐ MasterCard

Shipping & Handling charge from chart below	
Subtotal	
Please add applicable state & local sales tax	
TOTAL	

Account No. ☐☐☐☐☐☐☐☐☐☐☐☐☐☐☐☐☐☐

Signature _____ Exp. Date_____
Order invalid without signature

In a hurry? Call 1-800-822-8158 anytime, day or night, or visit your local bookstore.

Key = BC95ZZA

Shipping and Handling Charges

Order Amount	Within U.S.	Outside U.S.
Less than $15	$3.50	$5.50
$15.00 - $24.99	$4.00	$6.00
$25.00 - $49.99	$5.00	$7.00
$50.00 - $74.49	$6.00	$8.00
$75.00 - and up	$7.00	$9.00